HOOK, LINE, AND CLIFF HANGER

By A. J. Sieling

TABLE OF CONTENTS

INTRODUCTION

There are few techniques in writing quite as divisive as cliffhangers. Writers want to write them; readers hate to read them; and debates about their efficacy abound.

My personal feelings toward them have largely been neutral. I have read a few that bothered me, but, overall, if well done, I don't really notice and simply dive right into the next book in the series. And I certainly don't mind chapter-level cliffhangers. That said, for a long time, I never really played around with the idea of writing them myself.

But then one day, (insert dramatic music)... someone wrote this (paraphrased) review of one of my books on their personal blog. "This book ended on a cliffhanger, and I can't wait to read the next one!"

What?! I was baffled. Yeah, it was a short ending. I could agree with them there. But a *cliffhanger*? Assuming the reader didn't really know what a cliffhanger was, I put the review out of my mind and moved on with my life.

But the thing was, that reader was only the first to bring it up. And it turned out to not only be that book. The comments added up: a reader in a forum mentioning that cliffhanger in a different book I wrote, a person at an event commenting on another cliffhanger, another review referencing that damn cliffhanger-that-wasn't-a-cliffhanger yet again.

Never had I ever considered any of my book endings to be cliffhangers, nor was it my intention to have them perceived that way. The endless string of comments continued to mystify me. The only upside was that there didn't seem to be much anger toward my cliffhangers, despite the general attitude toward cliffhangers in the reading community.

Fast forward a few years, to when a traditionally published author I followed online released her first book. Her readers raved about it—including the *cliffhanger* at the end!

I couldn't believe it: a cliffhanger? And the readers *loved* it! It had them rushing out to preorder the next book the moment it was available.

Nearly every conversation I'd ever engaged in or witnessed regarding cliffhangers involved readers expressing their abject hatred for the literary device. But, somehow, this author had nailed a cliffhanger so well, their readers were clamoring for more, despite having to wait an entire year for the next book in the series. Obviously, I bought the book so I could make a determination for myself.

I formulated an opinion. And then bought another book with a cliffhanger ending. And another. And another. All with the intention of figuring what, exactly, a cliffhanger actually is.

I quickly realized the word "cliffhanger" was used to refer to a variety of different story- and scene-ending techniques, some of which are terribly frustrating and disappointing, and others which have us sitting on the edge of our seats and begging for more.

Readers hate being disappointed at the end of a story. But they love tension and suspense.

So what's the difference between a "good" cliffhanger and a "bad" one? How do we know what impact *our* cliffhanger will have on the reader? And how do we decide whether or not to use one at the end of a chapter or book?

This book is an attempt to explore this question in depth, look at various types of cliffhangers from a variety of angles, and give you enough information to help you decide how to end your book in a way that will satisfy your readers and lure them into the next book in the series—hook, line, and cliffhanger.

CHAPTER 1:
The Cliffs Edge

There's nothing quite like the feeling of being fully immersed in a story, turning the page, and then... nothing. The author has ended the book before you're ready for it to be over. On occasion I've wondered: was the book misprinted? Did they leave off the last chapter? Or did the writer do this to me... *on purpose*?

It's a strange mixture of disappointment and anticipation, followed by a flash of fury.

Why would the writer do this? What would possess them to rip away the conclusion to such a gripping tale? Were they trying to ruin my day?

Writers choose to craft stories for many reasons. Some of us love writing or storytelling. Some of us just "have a story inside that needs to come out." Some of us want to make money or have the title of "author." And there are many other reasons.

But one thing that makes writing stories so wonderful is that inherent within the process of doing so is a certain type of power: the power to give a reader an emotional experience.

We can make them laugh and cry, cause them to feel anxious or relaxed, or incite them to throw the book across the room. Sometimes, we can even help change a person's mind or influence their behavior in real life. In fact, if you participate in reader communities on social media or in person, or if you read reviews on books, you will notice the conversation often focuses on how a book made the reader *feel*.

"It was cute and funny!" they might say.

"This book had me sobbing at the end!"

"I was so ready for this book to be over. I wish I'd never read it."

"I loved this."

"I hated this."

"I wish I could read this book for the first time again."

Our stories make readers feel things.

This is a power. And a responsibility.

And how we choose to wield this power is entirely up to us. We might try to create warm and relaxing experiences for our readers. We might try to make them cry or rage. We might try to immerse them so thoroughly that they want to live in our stories. We might try to make them afraid or angry or deeply, desperately sad.

But I know that out of all the emotions readers might experience when reading my work, the last one I want to inflict upon them is *disappointment*. In my work or in me.

To be clear, I think sympathetic disappointment, where the reader feels disappointed because the *character* is disappointed, is good. That simply means the reader feels connected to the character, and all the other emotions the character experiences will be inflicted upon the reader as well.

But disappointment that drags the reader out of the story, or disappointment because the writer didn't deliver what they promised at the beginning of a narrative, or disappointment that breaks the fourth wall—that is what I want to avoid.

As writers, we have many tools that enable us to offer our readers emotional experiences: genres, tropes, characterization, plot structures, dialogue, and rhetorical devices, just to name a few. And which devices work best depends entirely on the reader and what type of experience they're looking for.

Cliffhangers are simply another device, another tool in our writer's toolbox. We can use them or not—it's up to us. And whether they will deliver a satisfying emotional experience will depend partially on the skill with which we wield them, and partially on the reader.

But even though much of the effect depends on the reader, it doesn't mean we can't write *better* cliffhangers. Or that we can't choose the best time and place for maximum emotional impact. Or that we can't do so in a way that leaves the reader desperate for more, rather than disappointed in the narrative (or in us).

My intention is to break down the different types of cliffhangers so we can see the effect each can have on a narrative, and thus on a reader; explore what kinds of emotional impacts can be delivered with these techniques; and delve a little deeper into this specific type of suspense.

We can learn to shove our readers over the cliff's edge on purpose—and have them enjoy the fall.

CHAPTER 2:
What Are Cliffhangers?

What are cliffhangers, exactly? If you go to the dictionary, which is a reasonable first place to check, you'll find some vague answers about stories or chapters with suspenseful endings. I checked multiple dictionaries and found answers like "a suspenseful situation," or "a situation of which the outcome is suspensefully uncertain until the last moment." But from the perspective of a writer, these definitions are next to useless. Because while many readers have strong feelings about cliffhangers, we know they don't hate *suspense*. They may have preferences about the intensity of the suspense or a particular technique. But suspense is something that keeps you riveted on the story, that makes you turn page after page, staying up late into the night and refusing to let your brain go to sleep.

So what is the difference between a cliffhanger that readers hate and a suspenseful ending that readers love?

In the writing community, we talk about other forms of suspense as being critical to crafting an engrossing narrative. Conflict and tension, for example, are touted as some of the most important elements of story—whether it's romantic conflict and tension, political conflict and tension, or action-based conflict and tension. At least in Western storytelling, we *need* suspense for a good story.

But conflict that seems contrived or easily solved can fall flat. Romances where the characters don't really seem to have anything in common can feel fake. Disagreements that could be fixed with a tiny amount of clear communication can be frustrating. This is because using a technique or trope doesn't guarantee a specific emotional reaction—it doesn't guarantee suspense. And when poorly executed, it can actually pull the reader out of the story, instead of dragging them deeper in.

Cliffhangers, similarly, are a useful technique that can drive story-level tension, but they can be difficult to pull off successfully. You want the reader to feel like they're standing at the edge of a precipice—and that's the key. The *edge* is where the tension is. Not tumbling into the abyss. If they're already falling, there's no more tension—they're already dead.

A well-constructed cliffhanger that leaves the reader hanging in all the *right* ways will have them turning the pages late into the night or reaching for the next book as soon as they've finished the previous one.

A poorly structured cliffhanger that leaves the reader hanging in all the *wrong* ways can have the opposite effect. It can cause the reader to put down the series and never return. It can even cause the reader to forego other books written by the same author because they want to avoid that sense of disappointment and frustration.

A good cliffhanger leaves the reader excited and desperate for more. A bad cliffhanger leaves the reader disappointed and upset.

Of course, "good" and "bad" are certainly subjective terms. No ending will give every reader the same emotional experience. And some readers just won't get it. That's okay! But it's certainly worth being aware of the type of emotional experience an ending is most likely to deliver.

Cliffhangers aren't limited to the endings of an entire book—we can also use them as a method for ending a chapter or a scene. I would argue that writers have a lot more leeway from the reader toward cliffhangers inside the book than cliffhangers at the end of the book. This is because, with chapter-level cliffhangers, if the reader wants to know what happens, they can just turn the page. Whereas with a cliffhanger at the end of a book, they have to wait for the next in the series—either until it's released, or until they can get their hands on a copy, which can sometimes be years, depending on the speed the author releases books.

A good cliffhanger should do at least some of the following things:

> ➤ Create a feeling of suspense and anticipation in the reader so they want to continue the story.

- ➤ Be relevant to the plot or the narrative. If something irrelevant happens, it typically feels forced. The exception to this rule is in something like absurdist fiction, where non sequiturs and ridiculous scenarios are part of the foundation of the subgenre.

- ➤ Be placed strategically and not thrown in because you don't know where to take the story or what to write next.

- ➤ Have foreshadowing, subtle or otherwise. This will allow the reader to suspect that *something* is going to happen, even if they don't know precisely what, stretching out that sense of suspense well before the cliffhanger actually arrives.

- ➤ Communicate clear stakes, so the reader knows exactly what the potential consequences of the situation could be. Without stakes, a cliffhanger isn't really a cliffhanger. It's just a story that ended too early.

- ➤ Promise resolution, so the reader trusts that whatever comes in the next scene or book will resolve their sense of anticipation. This promise is extremely important. If the reader doesn't trust you to deliver, they won't continue the story.

➤ Reveal a surprise that adds complexity and intrigue to the narrative. At a foundational level, the cliffhanger should at least surprise the reader. But beyond that, it can help to weave in additional details that either answer a previously asked question, or open new questions—ones the reader wants to know the answers to.

To the contrary, a bad cliffhanger is one which:

➤ Lacks genuine suspense, making the reader feel like the tension is either forced or easily resolved.

➤ Is an overused technique within a single narrative. If a novel-length book has a cliffhanger at the end of every single chapter and at the end as well, it's likely the reader will become fatigued by the repeated use of the same technique.

➤ Is incomplete or illogical. My personal feeling is that these are the most frustrating cliffhangers of all. They make me ask "why?" in a way that breaks the fourth wall by dragging me out of the narrative. It has me wondering about the *author* and their decisions, rather than the *character* and theirs.

➤ Feels forced or contrived. If the cliffhanger doesn't seem to arise naturally from the flow of the story, it feels like the author just stuck it in there to manipulate me into buying the book or turning the page—again, making me think about the author and their decisions, rather than the intentions of the character.

➤ Creates a total lack of resolution. *Something* needs to be resolved in a story, even if it's small, even if it's not the main plot or the biggest question posed at the beginning of the story.

The major theme here is that a good cliffhanger gives the reader a *desirable* emotional experience, while a bad cliffhanger gives the reader an *undesirable* emotional experience.

Readers enjoy feeling engaged with a story. They enjoy suspense, hope, fear, excitement, and wonder. They do not enjoy frustration, disappointment, and irritation. At least, not when those feelings are directed at the author, rather than the villain.

I want to pause just for a moment here and note that, of course, there will always be authors who don't care about any of this. Some authors don't care what the reader thinks. They don't care what editors think. They don't care what anyone thinks! They will do whatever the hell they want, and I'm all for it. These are not intended to be rules, just observations and suggestions.

The key is to understand *why* you're making the specific narrative decisions, so you have as much control as possible over the emotional experience you're creating for the reader as you develop the story.

Chapter-Level Cliffhangers

While most of this book focuses on cliffhangers placed at the end of a book, chapter-level cliffhangers can also be a useful and meaningful tactic to create suspense within a narrative. In each chapter, a story typically has at least three things: a character, a place, and movement. Movement could be one of several types:

- ➤ Spatial: when the character moves from one physical location to another.

- ➤ Emotional: when the character experiences a shift in their emotional state.

- ➤ Intellectual: when the character learns new information.

- ➤ Interpersonal: when the character's relationship with another character changes— such as meeting a new person, a deepening relationship, or disagreement.

- ➤ Internal: when the character changes their mind or primary objective.

- ➤ External: when something happens to the character that they did not initiate or plan for (acts of god, for example).

A chapter-level cliffhanger can appear several ways, but typically, it means that the outcome of the movement remains unknown; the chapter breaks before we find out how the shift impacts the character.

For example, if a character meets a new love interest, but their meet-cute is interrupted when the story shifts to a new chapter, you may not know how the new love interest felt about the meeting. This can create a sense of tension and anticipation for the reader—both of which are forms of suspense. Hopefully, the reader will turn the page to find out what happens. To draw out the tension, the author may even make the next chapter skip to a different viewpoint, delaying the reader's gratification to learn the outcome of the meeting.

This type of technique is an excellent way to add suspense within the story itself, and there are plenty of chapter-ending tropes that do this, for example:

- ➤ The character becomes unconscious.

- ➤ The lights go out.

- ➤ A catastrophe happens in the last paragraph.

- ➤ Something important is ripped away from the character in the last moments.

- ➤ Another character makes a surprising choice that the main character wasn't expecting.

- ➤ The character is left behind.

- ➤ An act of god happens in the last moments.

This list of tropes could go on for a long time. Many authors have used a wide range of chapter-level cliffhangers to create chapter-level suspense.

A strong chapter-level cliffhanger:

- ➤ Surprises the character, and hopefully the reader too.

- ➤ Makes sense within the context of the narrative.

- ➤ Creates a lack of resolution to the movement that happened within the chapter, but promises future resolution.

- ➤ Has clear stakes.

- ➤ Is placed strategically.

Avoid cliffhangers thrown in because the story feels boring or because you don't know what happens next.

And definitely avoid cliffhangers that don't make sense for the story you're writing.

The key to a successful chapter-level cliffhanger is surprise. If the reader can't guess what's coming, they're likely to remain hooked on the story—so long as the surprise twists and turns make sense within the context of the narrative. A contemporary romance novel in which aliens land and kidnap the love interest would not make sense. But in a sci-fi romance? Sounds epic.

CHAPTER 3:
Building a Mountain Range

Next I want to talk about cliffhangers at a series level, but to do so, I want to back up a little. The plot structure of a full narrative tends to be much more complex than the structure of a scene or chapter. So, to make sure we're on the same page, I'm going to do a high-level review of basic plot structure from both a series perspective and a single-book perspective.

Let's begin by visualizing a book series topographically, specifically as a mountain or hills. In this metaphor, each book in the series is a hill or a mountain. Some mountains stand alone, as individual peaks in the center of a field—like monadnocks. Others stand near each other, but remain distinct—like drumlins. And others still are interconnected so tightly that it's difficult to separate one from the other—like a mountain range.

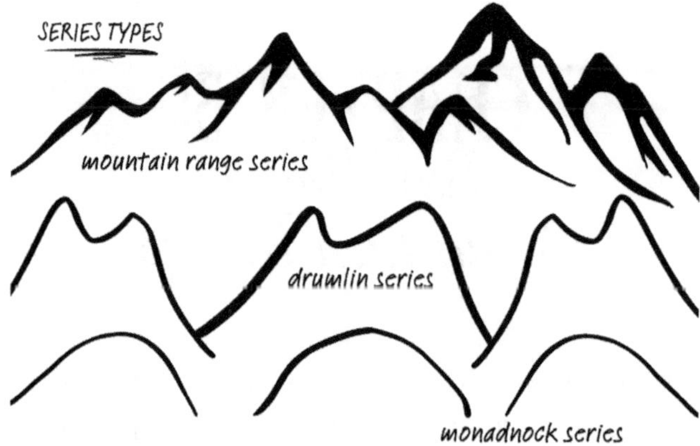

In a **monadnock** series, each book is distinct from the others. It is its own mountain, far apart from the others. It can be read and enjoyed, even if the reader doesn't realize it's part of a series.

Consider this book, the one you're reading right now: *Hook, Line, and Cliffhanger* by A. J. Sieling, Book 5 in the *Writers Reach* series. The other books in this series, while branded similarly and all written by me, have different approaches and are about very different topics. They're entirely *separate*, conceptually speaking. This book is not technically a standalone, but it could be. It is part of a monadnock series.

In television, you might see this structure in an anthology show, like *Black Mirror, Twilight Zone,* or *American Horror Story.* Each episode stands on its own; you don't have to watch them in order to understand and appreciate each. They are related, but do not rely on each other for the story to make sense.

In a **drumlin** series, on the other hand, there is a small amount of overlap. Consider a romance series in which each book has its own main characters with their own love story; each book can easily be read on its own. There's no need to delve into the other books in the series if you don't want to—the story is whole and complete by itself. You can read the books in any order. *But,* there is still a lot more connection between the stories than in a monadnock series. You may have overlapping settings, family members or other characters, or maybe even a background "situation" that affects each of the characters differently. The books in the series are like drumlins, each individually distinct, but still *threaded together* deliberately and intentionally.

This is a common series structure in contemporary romance, historical romance, steampunk romance, and fantasy romance, as well as in mystery and thriller. Terry Pratchett's *Discworld* series may also be a good example of this. And, in television, it's a very common technique in sitcoms and adult animated shows—*Friends* or *Futurama*, for example. There is overlap—the same characters and settings—but you can watch most of the episodes in pretty much any order.

In a **mountain range** series, the books *must be read in order*. They are intricately tied together—the plots and the subplots rely on one another. The smaller mountains support the bigger mountains. While each book may have its own climactic moment—its own highest peak—it's so tightly woven with the plots of the other books, they can't be separated from each other. In order to understand Books 4, 5, and 6, you have to read Books 1, 2, and 3 first. They are *inseparable* from one another.

This is very common in science fiction and fantasy genres. Think *Mistborn* by Brandon Sanderson, *Lord of the Rings* by J. R. R. Tolkien, or *Throne of Glass* by Sarah Maas. In television, this is also a very common strategy—you can see it in shows like *Game of Thrones*, *Umbrella Academy*, *The Good Place*, *Silo*, *Continuum*, and *Dark Matter*, to name a few.

To be clear, I think there is plenty of gray area in between each of these categories—not to mention, how you perceive a series is likely to be entirely subjective. Some series are somewhere in between a monadnock and a drumlin (for example, *Family Guy*); some are a small mountain range (a procedural like *NCIS*, for example), and others a big mountain range (*Sword of Truth* series by Terry Goodkind); and, for all I know, some writers may prefer to visualize their series as an ocean or caves or some completely different geographical feature. Trees maybe. Or a town. Rivers. In addition, one reader might think of a series as one type, while the author intended to write a different type.

This flexibility isn't super important in the grand scheme of things. These categories aren't meant to be exclusive or rigid, but just to provide a framework for talking about the shape of a story, and in our case specifically, in the context of cliffhangers.

It's also important to mention that scenes can also be talked about using this metaphor. Some books have separate and distinct scenes, like monadnocks, sometimes even with varying characters or sizeable gaps of time between them. Some books can even form a series of what seem like entirely isolated moments, where you can't see the connections until later in the book or the very end—here I'm thinking of something like *Dirk Gently's Holistic Detective Agency* by Douglas Adams.

Other authors write scenes that flow into each other like an interconnected mountain range (or tributaries to a river). And some authors find a space somewhere in the middle, separating out chapters or using scene breaks to create more or less space between the important moments within the narrative. Like drumlins or rolling hills.

Story Arcs Are Shaped Like Hills

Now I want to narrow in on a single story, as opposed to series or scenes. The reason I like the geography/mountain metaphor so much is because I think it fits nicely with the way we already talk about story structure within a singular narrative.

The generic plot beats for most narratives typically look something like this:

➤ **Exposition:** This is the beginning of the story, where the characters, setting, and key plot details are introduced to the reader.

➤ **Rising Action:** This is where the events in the story pick up. The character/s experience challenges and are actively facing the fundamental conflict of the story.

➤ **Climax:** This is the moment where the character faces the main test or conflict of the story. Sometimes they win; sometimes they don't.

➤ **Falling Action:** This happens after the climax, in which the character has to face the consequences of the decisions they made during the climactic moment.

➤ **Resolution:** This is when the conflict is fully resolved. "Resolved" doesn't necessarily mean fixed; rather, it means we find out whether the character got what they wanted or achieved their goal. Sometimes they might not get what they want, but instead have a realization about how to get it, or they might realize they actually want something else—this is a common series tactic that typically feeds into the larger series plot.

Now, if I make a sketch of each of these elements—look! Another mountain!

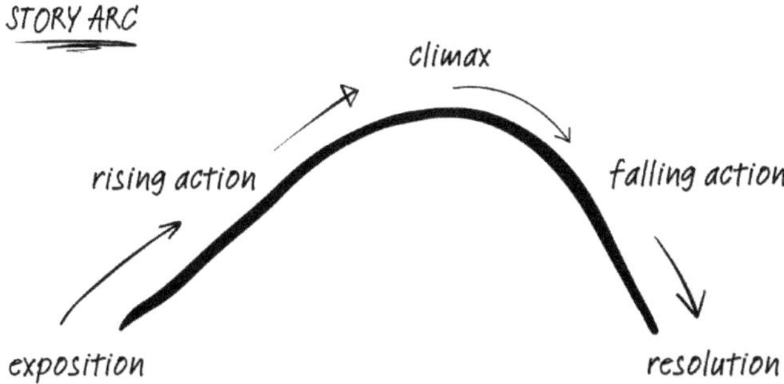

The story arc begins with exposition and leads into the rising action, then culminates with the climax, which is followed by the falling action and, ultimately, the resolution.

Of course, this is only the most basic plot structure out there. There are plenty of other methods for structuring a plot. For example, you may be familiar with the Hero's Journey, Heroine's Journey, Save the Cat, the Snowball Method, the Three-Act Structure, Freytag's Pyramid, or any of the others—these can all be visualized into some kind of hill or mountain if you so choose (even Hero's & Heroine's Journey, though they are typically represented as a circle).

You can also think of plot structure across an entire series, at least with a mountain range series. For example, in some epic fantasy series that use the Hero's Journey plot structure, the main character doesn't "Cross the Threshold" or become "Master of Two Worlds" until the very last book in the series. Each book may follow a more generic plot structure with rising action, a climactic moment near the end, and a denouement, but the specific beats of the Hero's Journey actually play out over the course of the series as a whole.

This means you may have a series that looks a bit more like this:

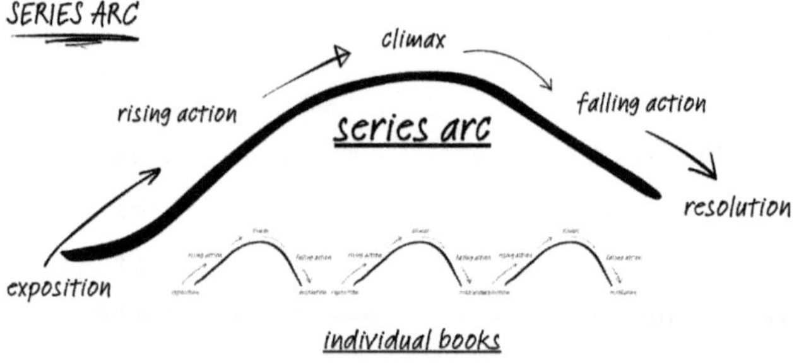

In this image, you can see that each individual book has its own arc, but together, they add up to the larger arc of the series. In my experience, the series exposition is typically in the first book; the series climax, series falling action, and series resolution tend to all be in the last book; and all the books in between would land in the "rising action" category. Though that's not to say you couldn't do it however you wanted.

You may also find that some very long series have multiple series arcs, either one right after another, or layered beneath one another. Again, it's quite subjective.

It's all about how you perceive the rising and falling action and tension of a book or series.

In my view, mountain range series tend to have the series arc most obviously applied. Monadnock series likely don't have them, or if they do, they're less apparent until the end. And drumlin series can have them, but the individual narratives are tied together much more loosely, so when you step back, you're more likely to see rolling hills than a soaring mountain range.

This means that mountain range series are also the most likely to incorporate cliffhangers as a technique to create tension within the overarching series.

There are lots of ways to think about crafting series. Weaving is a good metaphor, or sculpting—maybe even cooking. But since we're going to be diving into cliffhangers, geography ties in nicely, and makes for additional metaphors for pathways and routes that individual or multiple characters can take as they move through their stories.

Emotional Impact of Series Types

One of the primary goals in creating a story is to leave the reader with an emotional experience. But to fully understand the emotional impact of a cliffhanger, we first have to understand the most likely emotional impact of the different types of series.

Emotional impact can happen at any point in a series. Some readers respond to single, tiny moments within a story. Some readers respond to specific tropes. Other readers are more focused on the climactic moment or specific events that impact a character. But, ultimately, the story can create the strongest, most powerful emotional response in a reader at the climactic moment, by weaving character, tension, pacing, suspense, setting, and all the elements of story—and then delivering a meaningful, impactful resolution to the challenges faced by the characters.

But how this plays out varies in part based on series type.

Monadnock Single-Day Hike

With monadnock series, the reader is getting all of their emotional satisfaction at once. The rising action, climax, and resolution all come within one book. Whatever emotional experience the reader hoped for is gained during the two or three or ten hours they spent reading that book. And they understand that if they pick up a different book in the series, they might get a completely different emotional experience.

The series you're currently reading, *Writers Reach,* is a good example. Let's assume that when you reach the end of this book, *Hook, Line, and Cliffhanger,* it provided an intellectually satisfying experience for you. You may choose to pick up another book in the series, but there's no guarantee it will offer the same experience—perhaps you love my approach to the craft of writing but hate my approach to marketing and branding. The expectation is that each book *may* offer a similar experience, but it also may not. Because they're different books on different topics. Monadnocks.

A fictional example of this might include Diana Wynne Jones's *Howl Series*, which includes *Howl's Moving Castle, Castle in the Air*, and *House of Many Ways*, which are so loosely linked, they are like standalones, despite being set in the same world. They also (from my very subjective reader's perspective) offer quite different emotional experiences, even if they are all enjoyable and satisfying.

Drumlin Exploration

With a drumlin series, the reader will get *most* of their emotional satisfaction from a single book, but there may be threads or subplots that remain unresolved, which drive the reader to the next book in the series—a new view from the top of a different drumlin, so to speak. In a regency romance, for example, perhaps the main character's sister has an intriguing story waiting to be consumed in the second book of the series, though the romance is fully complete in the first book. Or in a fantasy series like *Discworld* by Terry Pratchett, perhaps you want to find out what's happening with the wizards or the witches or in a completely different city in the world. They are linked by living in the same world and having crossover situations and characters, but most of the books do not rely on each other to be entertaining and satisfying reads.

Each narrative delivers its own sense of emotional satisfaction, but there is also an emotional pull toward the other books in the series, leaving you with the hope you'll find some more questions answered when you pick up another book in the series.

Mountain Range Trek

With a mountain range series, the full satisfaction doesn't come until the very end. Sure, curiosity may be temporarily sated by each book in the series—you get to learn *something* about the character, world, or conflict, but the expectation is that you have to wait until you've read the final book to get the full emotional experience of the narrative. There are many popular series like this, such as any of Sarah Maas' series, Tamora Pierce's quartets, *Lord of the Rings* by Tolkien, or *Wheel of Time* by Robert Jordan.

These stories take the reader on a long and winding emotional journey through book after book, offering a wide range of emotional experiences at both a micro and a macro level. Ideally, however, when the reader reaches the final climactic moment, they will experience the most satisfying emotional impact, and leave the story feeling sated and fulfilled.

The Emotional Impact of A Cliffhanger

The emotional impact of a story is driven by many factors, ranging from tension and pacing, to genre and tropes. A tool like a cliffhanger gives us a way to create a specific type of emotional experience for the reader, but may also fall flat and drive the reader out of the story.

If the goal is to create a sense of suspense for the reader, then we have to walk that fine line of giving the reader enough information and satisfaction to keep them immersed in the story, while also withholding key details or scenes to make them want to keep going. Cliffhangers are a classic method of withholding information, but it's important to ask yourself: *How will withholding this information affect the reader's emotional experience of the story?*

Imagine a romance novel that is filled with romantic tension—sideways glances, barely withheld desire, and deep longing between the love interests. Then, the book ends on a cliffhanger with no romantic resolution of any kind—the characters don't clearly fall in love, no kiss, no sex scene, nothing. This would likely disappoint the reader a great deal, even to the point of infuriating them. Sometimes certain types of scenes are withheld until the next book—for example, many romance series level up the steam in each book by having a profession of affection in the first book, a kiss in the second book, and sex in the third book. But if the reader gets *no resolution of any kind*, they are likely to be minimally disappointed—and some might argue it wasn't a romance at all.

In fact, there is some debate in the romance community about whether a romance novel with a cliffhanger even counts as romance. Technically, a romance only has to have two characteristics for it to count in the genre: falling in love and a happy ending. But there are plenty of romance writers who occasionally include cliffhanger endings in their story—either because it's right for the story or because they're confident it will deliver a specific type of emotional experience.

The same thing is true for other genres of story: conflicts need *some* kind of resolution, even if it's just a tactic for pushing the full resolution off to the next book. When crafting a cliffhanger, even if your goal is to create suspense by leaving the reader hanging, it's important to leave at least a small resolution in order to keep the reader emotionally engaged until they can get the next book in the series.

CHAPTER 4:
The Truncate

There are five types of cliffhangers that I want to talk about in this book, and the first is what I call a "Truncate Cliffhanger."

The word "truncate" means to shorten as if by cutting off. For example, when you want to make a long video clip shorter by removing the ending, you truncate it. Data truncation is when data is stored somewhere too short or small to contain the entirety of it, so it gets cut off. And in mathematics, if you have a long decimal number, you might truncate it by removing all digits after a certain point. For example, Pi is usually truncated at 3.14 even though the number is infinite and could be truncated in lots of places: 3.14159265358979323...

A Truncate Cliffhanger is much the same. It is when a story is ended too soon or too early; when it's cut off without resolution. To my mind, this would be either before or in the middle of the climax, **leaving no falling action or resolution of any kind.**

Let's return for a moment to our story arc visual, but this time, we'll include a Truncate Cliffhanger.

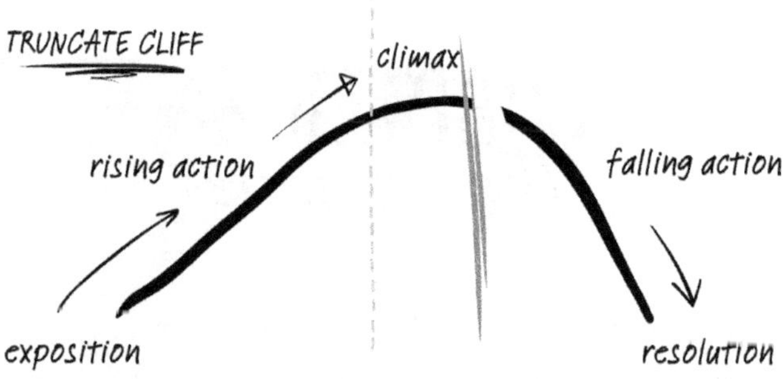

As you can see, the story progresses through the exposition and rising action, all the way to the climactic moment. Then, at some point *before or during* the climactic moment, the story cuts off, sending the reader tumbling headlong over the metaphorical cliff.

There are a couple of reasons a writer might make this choice.

The first is when it seems as though the writer doesn't entirely know where the story is going. So they just end it and hope they figure it out in the next book.

The second is when they hope that leaving the reader hanging at the critical moment will force them to run out and buy the next book. Sometimes this works, and sometimes it doesn't. Make sure you know your audience if you want to attempt it. I'll also mention that this may be a more reasonable tactic if the book is already quite long, and you've given your reader many, many opportunities to become invested in the character, world, and story.

The third reason is when the story arc lends itself to a *sub-climactic moment* (I'll get more into this shortly), but then cuts off after that, without resolving the primary conflict in the book. This would be a pre-climactic truncate.

And then occasionally, there are books when the story just... ends, with no apparent relation to the story structure. The reader is not entirely sure why the author made that decision. There seems to be no obvious reason—uncertainty, marketing, subplots, or anything.

These seem to be the type of cliffhangers readers hate the most. They are frustrating, offering no emotional resolution. Often, the reader feels like they've been cheated or ripped off. If angry enough, they may not simply book put down the book, but never pick up another book by the same author again.

Mid-Climax Truncates

In a story that has a single climactic moment, the reader spends the entire book looking forward to that point of the narrative: here is where they find out what happens. Who did it? Who ended up with whom? What is the meaning of life, the universe, and everything? *Who dies?*

The climax is where they will find out how the character's arc resolves, how the big question is answered, how the main conflict is resolved. They find out whether the main character achieves their goal, and, more importantly, *how* they achieve it. It is the moment where all is revealed, the battle is fought, and the enemy is defeated (or not).

Mostly, though, this is the moment of the narrative where the emotional impact of the story hits home. Everything the reader was hoping for happens here. It is the moment they've been anticipating, the reason they kept turning page after page.

Not all books end the way we want them to, of course, and sometimes the climax doesn't deliver the emotional impact we'd hoped for, even if everything is wrapped up neatly and makes sense at the end.

Not every published book is the best book ever, and that's okay.

But when the narrative ends *mid*-climax, the reader can sometimes feel cheated. What happened? Who won the battle? Who felled the boss? Who did they end up with romantically? Who died? And how did the protagonist feel after completing their mission or quest?

And if the author won't tell us now, will we ever find out? What if they never finish the series? Looking at you, George.

An easy example of this type of ending is from the TV show *Friends*. You've probably heard of it.

Let's fast forward to Season 3, Episode 25, titled "The One at the Beach." In earlier seasons, the main characters Ross and Rachel dated; then they had a fight, Ross hooked up with someone else, and they broke up.

Now, later, Ross has a new girlfriend, Bonnie, but he still has feelings for Rachel.

At the very end of the episode, Ross is standing in a hallway, glancing back and forth between two doors. Behind one door, he will find Rachel. Behind the other door, Bonnie. He picks one door—but the audience doesn't know who is behind it.

And then the episode is over.

What happened? Who did he choose? Whose room did he enter? What inspired him to decide? Did he decide to choose love (Rachel)? Or did he choose to move on with his life (Bonnie)?

This kind of truncate cliffhanger can definitely leave the reader (or watcher) feeling unfulfilled. At the same time, it can spur debate, discussion, and thoughts about the ending and why the writers made that choice.

You get to decide what's right for your story and your audience. But if you opt to go with this sort of risky technique, make sure you do so intentionally, know what emotional response you're hoping for from your readers—and be aware of how readers may react if it falls flat for them.

Pre-Climax Truncates

Let's take a slight detour for a moment to talk about cliffhangers that occur *before* the climax. Typically, this is a strategy used when a book has a sub-climax, which is a moment within a narrative that feels like a climactic moment in some ways—it usually has high action, intense decision-making, or heightened conflict—but it is still leading toward the main conflict. A sub-climax will not answer the key question asked at the beginning of the book, and it will not offer any resolution to the primary plot. Often, the sub-climax can feel like a win for the main character, but it quickly turns into a loss.

In a romance novel, this might be the moment when the two lovers first come together, but before the main conflict drives them apart in the "break-up" moment. In fantasy, the main character might fight and win what they think is a major battle (that battle would be the sub-climax), but quickly realize they lost something crucial in the process, and that a bigger battle still lies ahead. In mystery, the sleuth might think they've solved the puzzle—and then realize they were wrong about a critical detail.

I want to mention here that this is a highly subjective experience. Different people experience the rise and fall of a narrative differently, so whether a book has a "sub-climax" at all is up to you, the reader. Even if you're *writing* the book, and you intentionally include a sub-climax, not everyone might experience it that way.

A singular narrative arc with a sub-climax could be visualized like this:

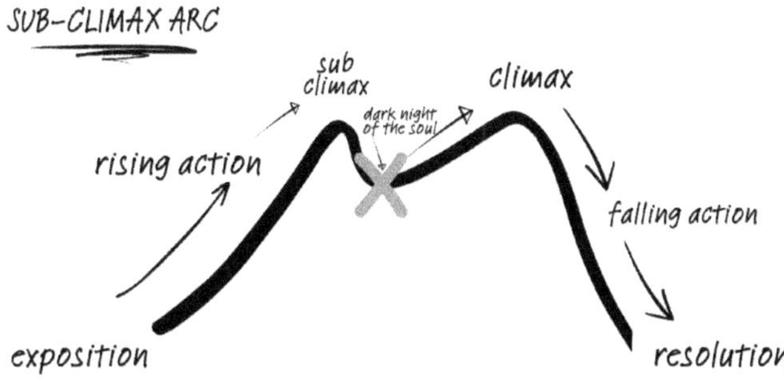

In this image, the exposition and rising action lead to a sub-climax. At this moment in the narrative, the main character usually *thinks* they are facing their biggest challenge, and often succeed, but just barely or with substantial loss. However, once they make it through the ordeal, they immediately realize it was not actually their biggest challenge, and instead, a more momentous conflict still awaits.

This typically drives the character to the "dark night of the soul" moment (as it's called in the Save the Cat story structure), which might also be part of the "Ordeal," or called the "All Is Lost" or the "Lowest Point" moment, depending on which plot structure you are using for your story.

If the story ends just after the initial mini-climax, when the character is in the depths of their moment of despair, I would also consider it a truncated cliffhanger, as shown in the image below, because it comes *before* the main climax.

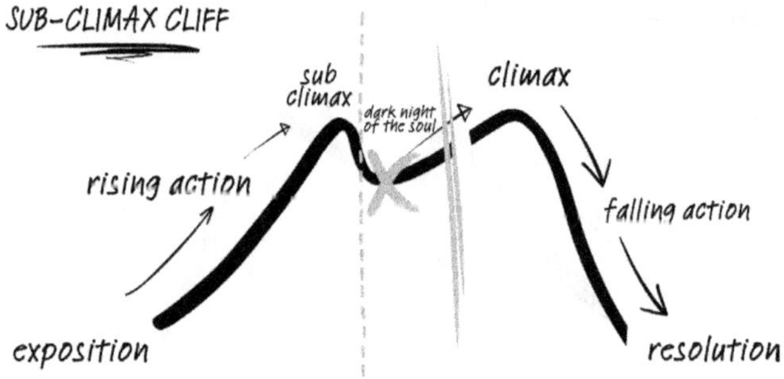

This type of ending is likely to be frustrating at best. It ends too early and doesn't offer any resolution to the conflicts the characters have been facing throughout the course of the story. It's tricky, though, because this is also often a series-level technique, which, when done well, can keep the reader grasping for the next installment.

A popular example of this type of cliffhanger is in *Cinder*, Book 1 of the *Lunar Chronicles* by Marissa Meyers. Again, this is a subjective interpretation of the story. I'll also note this sudden ending didn't bother most of her readers, as the books have been quite successful, but often, this type of ending is infuriating because it doesn't answer any of the questions asked by the reader.

(Spoilers ahead!)

Cinder is a science-fiction retelling of *Cinderella*, set in New Beijing after World War IV. The protagonist, Linh, is a cyborg mechanic with a robotic leg. A deadly plague is sweeping the city, and her younger sister contracts the illness. Throughout the course of the novel, however, Cinder discovers she is, in fact, immune to the virus. There is a romantic subplot, wherein Cinder meets the prince, who is dealing with a lunar colony that wants to wage war on Earth. He is the only thing standing in the way—and his only current option to prevent war is to marry the Lunar Queen.

There are many moving pieces to this story, but eventually, the various plotlines coincide at the annual ball, true to the Cinderella tale. Linh attends to warn the prince of the queen's true plan, which she stumbles across by accident. But at the ball, she learns her own true identity—that she is the missing Lunar princess. Linh is arrested and deposited in the palace prison, where she is forced to contemplate this new identity and the fate she now faces. She has lost everything, including her family, her home, her identity, and the prince in a classic dark night of the soul moment—and the story ends there.

It feels to me like a sub-climactic moment, when she's just faced the first big challenge, only to realize she still faces much, much bigger challenges ahead, and not only that, but she has no idea how to handle them. This feeling was especially strong for me since this was a Cinderella retelling. I thought she would escape and the prince would come looking for her. And perhaps this happens later in the series. But, to me, it felt like a cliffhanger delivered too early.

This is an example of when this type of cliffhanger can work, because it leads into the rest of the series—if you trust the author to deliver more emotional satisfaction later in the series. One advantage *Cinder* has is that the book is quite long, giving the reader plenty of time to get emotionally invested in the world and characters, despite the lack of resolution at the end. And, of course, this series has been quite successful, so the tactic mostly worked as intended.

It is also an example of how it might not work, since I (and lots of other readers) opted not to continue reading because of this narrative choice.

When To Use A Truncate Cliff

So when should you use truncate cliffhangers? When can they work?

Generally speaking, I'd say this type of cliffhanger is the most difficult to pull off successfully because often, the reader feels cheated—they were waiting for the main climax or the resolution, and it was ripped away from them at the last second.

But it can also be an engaging lead-in to the next book in the series that drives interest and enhances the emotional experience of the narrative, if the reader fully buys into the world and characters.

I'd also suggest that truncate cliffs are better used at the end of a book, and less commonly used to end a scene, specifically because scene arcs don't require a climactic moment for them to be meaningful and relevant, whereas most books do (note that I said *most* books, if you find yourself arguing with me in your head, lol), and a truncate ends the story during or before the climactic moment. Not that it can't be done; it's just far less common.

Here are a few scenarios for which using a truncate cliffhanger might be right for your series:

➤ When the book is already very long. A long book offers a few things to a reader that shorter books don't—a fully immersive world, complex and engaging characters you've had plenty of time to get to know, and a variety of trope-based emotional experiences to get you fully hooked on the story. A longer story has lots of opportunities for the reader to feel fully consumed by the tale, and a truncate cliffhanger is more likely to make them desperate for the next book, rather than frustrated that they didn't get what they were looking for.

➤ When the next book picks up right where the first book left off. Starting the next book elsewhere when the previous book was a truncate is a risky strategy, because the reader might feel cheated—like you made a promise and didn't deliver. Truncating the story and then picking up right where you left off enables the reader to trust that they're going to eventually get what you promised in book one, even if they have to wait longer for satisfaction.

➤ When you just *know* it's right for the story. There may be times when you instinctively know a truncate cliffhanger is the right choice for that story. In this case, trust your gut. Writing is a deeply subconscious process, and sometimes you just know something is right, even if you're risking upsetting readers or breaking the "rules." So go for it.

To the contrary, there are plenty of reasons to skip the cliffhanger. A few might be:

➤ It's not right for the genre.

➤ It's not right for the book.

➤ It's a standalone novel, or part of a drumlin or monadnock series.

➤ You know your specific subset of readers will be unhappy with the decision.

➤ You're not sure what comes next in the story, so you just end it.

➤ You're using it for its shock value to surprise your readers, rather than to create an immersive emotional experience.

Truncate cliffhangers can sometimes be effective. But they are a tricky choice, and one that requires careful thought and consideration. Ultimately, it doesn't matter what choice you make, there will always be some readers who don't like it. In the end, it comes down to what's right for your story.

CHAPTER 5:
The Embankment

On my twenty-first birthday, I was going for a walk, completely sober, and fell down an embankment. I hit several trees, and in the process of trying to avoid making it all the way to the bottom and landing in the stream, I somehow snapped a ligament in my ankle. I ended up spending the day in the ER and then being carried around campus by my friends.

It was a painful experience—and not one I'd like to relive. But it was exciting. And it definitely made that birthday one to remember.

I think Embankment Cliffhangers often offer a similar experience to a reader: a lot of pain but also a lot of excitement. An Embankment Cliffhanger can

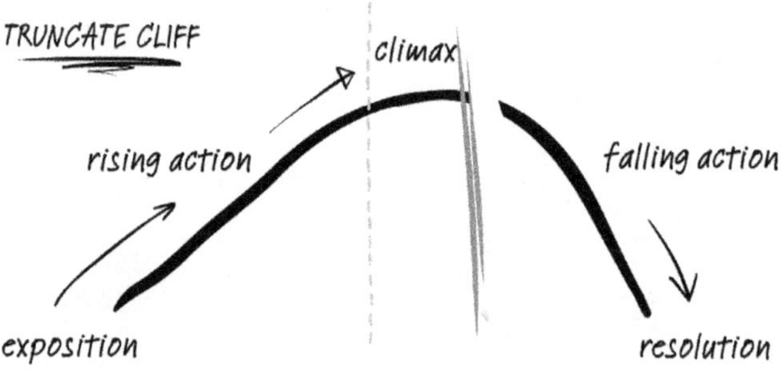

often look and feel like a cliff, but it offers something a little more than a Truncate Cliffhanger—it offers a path forward.

Let's take another look at our story arc, and this time, compare a Truncate Cliff to an Embankment.

Where the truncate cliff cuts before or during the climactic moment with no additional falling action or resolution, the embankment cliffhanger ends *post* climax, and offers *some* falling action. In this instance, however, any falling action is brief, and resolution is minimal. It goes right from the climactic moment to *The End*.

In my experience, these types of cliffhangers are better received by readers than truncate cliffhangers because the reader gets *something* at the end of the story, even if it's not everything they wanted. Often there are many, many threads left unresolved—any romances are typically left hanging, you rarely know the full implications of the outcome of the climax, and most of the

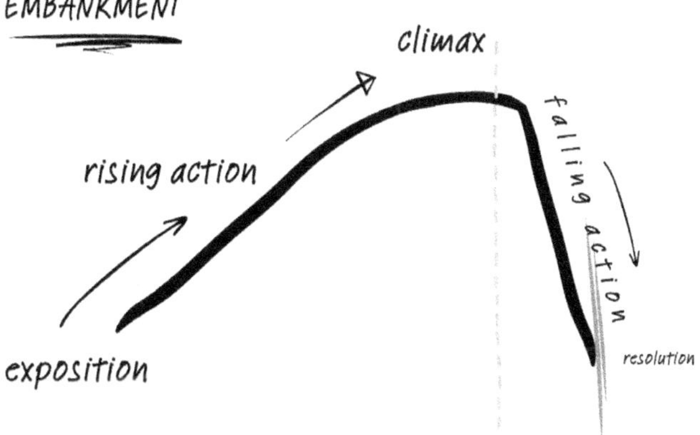

major and minor conflicts in the narrative have also not been resolved.

But because *some* resolution is offered, it's a slightly less frustrating method of ending a book. It's more like a compromise; you're saying, "I'm not going to tell you much, but here's a little something to keep you engaged until the next book."

I like to use my book, *City of Dod*, as an example of this type of cliffhanger. *City of Dod* is Book 2 in the *Land of Szornyek* series.

(Spoilers ahead!)

In this book, the main character, Askari, is living in a post-apocalyptic world filled with monsters. She is on the run from a pretty vicious creature, and, eventually, she and two friends end up in a run-down city called Dod, which is filled with a hallucinogenic fog. While there, they encounter a brand-new type of human-looking monster who traps them, intending to make them his next meal.

They are rescued, barely alive, from the city by some warriors from a community hunting this monster, and once they have recuperated, end up traveling back to Dod in search of a community member who has been kidnapped by this same creature. They come upon a strange research facility hidden in the fog, inside of which is a portal to another dimension from which dozens of new monsters are flooding.

This is the climactic moment. Their goal is to kill the monster they are hunting and rescue their friend. Alas—poor Yorick—they cannot kill the monster, and rather than saving their friend, she dies.

The book ends as they are fleeing from the research facility.

In this instance, the "resolution" offered to the reader is that they find out what happens to the friend who was kidnapped, though it is an unfortunate ending for her. But the big bad escapes, and the main character and her companions are once again left injured and fleeing for their lives. The reader doesn't find out how the main character feels about their recent encounter, or what they are going to do next—they simply fight the bad guy, and then the book ends.

There are maybe three pages before the big climactic scene and the end of the book. It is a sudden and abrupt ending—an embankment.

I offered an olive branch by resolving one of the key threads of the book, but also ripped out the rug from underneath the reader by leaving the characters injured in a dangerous situation, with a new and deadly monster still on the loose.

This is one book my readers have referred to as a cliffhanger. This surprised me, but I can see it—even though the book completes the climactic moment and answers the question asked at the beginning of the tale. The ending is sharp and sudden, and definitely leaves the reader wanting more.

When To Use An Embankment

I'd say this type of cliffhanger is easier than the truncate to pull off successfully. Because you are offering something in return, even if it's just a small resolution to a single problem, the reader is a lot less likely to feel cheated by the outcome of the story, and more likely to be interested enough to pick up the next book in the series.

Embankment endings are excellent chapter endings as well—perhaps somewhat abrupt, but with a clear indication that some resolution is going to be coming sooner than later. You leave the scene in media res with one problem solved but a dozen remaining.

Here are a few scenarios for which using an embankment cliffhanger might be right for your series:

➤ To create suspense: Embankments, when well done, are the queens of suspense. They keep a reader on the edge of their seat, desperate to know what's going to happen. This can keep the reader turning the page or have them rushing out to pick up a copy of the next book in the series.

➤ To emphasize a sense of urgency: When the pace of the story is picking up, and you want your reader to feel like they're being sucked into the story and everything is about to come undone at the seams, this type of cliffhanger can accomplish that. Keeping the prose tight and the important moments crunched together can exacerbate that heightened sense of urgency and keep the doom clock in your reader's head ticking.

➤ To explore character development or deepen threads: By leaving some questions unanswered and weighted with unresolved tension, you can leave it open-ended as to what questions you're going to answer and how the character will grow in future installments.

➤ When you want to reflect a theme: Sometimes an embankment cliffhanger can structurally reflect a theme you're exploring in the manuscript—such as unresolved tension between people, lack of closure, or the unexpected twists and turns of life.

➤ When you just know it's right for the story; I know I said this in the last chapter, but it holds true here. Sometimes you just know. And, when you know, you know. Trust your gut.

In terms of when to skip an embankment cliffhanger:

- ➤ It's not right for the genre.

- ➤ It's not right for the book.

- ➤ You've already used several of the same type of cliffhanger at the end of scenes throughout the story.

- ➤ If it is a standalone monadnock or drumlin book—don't do this to your reader! If there won't be any additional books from that character's perspective, at least give them enough resolution to feel satisfied with the ending.

- ➤ For shock value. Even if the reader didn't fully expect an embankment, they should at least feel like it made sense for the story.

I'm sure there are other use cases for and against embankment cliffhangers, but again, in the end, it comes down to what you want, and what's right for the story.

CHAPTER 6:
The Flabbergast

Have you ever watched a dog run into a sliding glass door? One time, our 160lb Great Pyrenees, Blueberry, sprinted full speed toward the screen door. It popped right off, flew thirty feet, and landed on the other side of his fenced-in yard.

Aside from this being hilariously slapstick, it is a great metaphor for the Flabbergast Cliffhanger—which is arguably not a cliffhanger at all.

A Flabbergast Cliffhanger is simply when something surprising and unexpected happens right at the end of the story. It makes sense for the story, but is so unexpected, it leaves the reader flabbergasted.

Here, I made a diagram, even if it probably doesn't need one:

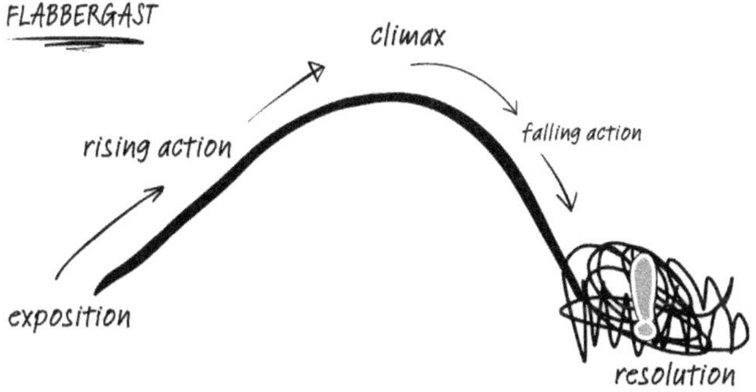

In a flabbergast, the reader gets all their favorite parts of a story. The exposition, the rising action, the climax, the falling action, the resolution. They get character arcs and world building, sub-climaxes and dark nights of the soul. They get everything they love—including all the key questions of the story answered, relationships formed, challenges overcome.

And then, in the very last minute, like a lightning bolt from Zeus: BAM! Something so surprising and unexpected happens, the reader is left looking for more pages in the book like they can't breathe without them.

This method only works if the reader has well and truly fallen in love with the characters and the world. Likely, if you succeed with a flabbergast, your reader will hate you, but in a good way.

The reason this works is not because the reader is surprised by the twist but because the *character* is. If the reader is empathizing with the character, and then the character is jerked sideways by a sudden change of plans, then the reader will get dragged on an emotional experience right along with them.

This is the best kind of emotional experience, in my opinion, when you're empathizing so deeply with the character that you simply can't handle sudden disasters, catastrophes, and WTFs. They leave you gasping, crying, desperately begging for more pages in the book.

My current favorite example of a flabbergast is the book *Ledge* by Stacey McEwan.

(Spoilers ahead!)

In *Ledge*, the main character, Dawsyn, lives on a frigid mountain, trapped by a gaping chasm, and a species called the Glacians come to collect a human sacrifice every season. At the beginning of the story, Dawsyn is finally selected as a sacrifice, after years of being overlooked, but through a series of wily risks and surprising aid, escapes down the mountain to where the rest of humanity lives in relative comfort, mostly safe from the vicious and terrifying Glacians.

A particular Glacian named Ryon, who is, of course, god-like in his handsomeness (insert romantic subplot here), aids her in her quest, and once she has escaped, she is determined to get to the human queens and demand they rescue the rest of Dawsyn's people from up on the Ledge.

Fast forward through most of the rising action to the main conflict, during which she faces down the queens of the realm. I won't spoil all the fun bits and bobs of the end sequence, only the part relevant to this type of cliffhanger.

Dawsyn thinks she has come out ahead of where she started. She hopes the queens will aid her. Due to the steps she has taken and the facts she has learned, it looks like her people will be saved. And then, in the last moments of the book, she finds out that Ryon (maybe) betrayed her, and then the queen stabs him... and he dies.

Talk about a whack on the side of the head.

It was completely out of left field, if you like sports metaphors.

And from what I can tell from the reviews, her readers absolutely ate it up. They were devastated. Crushed. Ripped apart from the inside out—and they loved every second.

The reason I think this works is that it gave the readers everything they wanted. It gave them answers to the big questions in the story. The motivations of the different players were revealed. The main character makes huge strides toward solving the problem. It felt good—it felt *right*. It felt like Dawsyn had achieved what she needed, at least for this moment in the series arc.

Except for—it was all a lie.

All the parts we want in a story are there: the exposition, rising action, climax, falling action—but the resolution is an absolutely bonkers whack to the side of the head. But it is still a resolution—and a resolution that makes the reader want to storm into the streets demanding that Book 2 be published ASAP.

When To Use A Flabbergast

I want to make something clear here: a flabbergast only works if the reader *trusts* the author. This is one of those techniques, in my opinion, that can only be used once in a narrative. If it's done too many times, the reader can feel like they're being jerked around.

This is not to say you can't have more than one surprise in a book. But the other surprises need to have some falling action, some resolution, some time for contemplation—the reader has to understand what's going on and why.

Typically, this would be tricky to pull off as a scene or chapter end, because the reader knows the narrative will come back to it eventually, and so it will have less impact than at the end of a book. But it can definitely be done.

I would also suggest that you could use a flabbergast not just in mountain range series, but also in drumlin series. In a drumlin series, where the story mostly stands alone, the flabbergast might set the reader up for the beginning of another book with a different character in a different place. The flabbergast might serve as the thread that connects the books together, even if they otherwise have nothing in common.

Here are a few scenarios when a flabbergast cliffhanger might be right for your series:

➤ To create a profound or deeply impactful emotional experience for the reader. Flabbergasts tend to be engaging and surprising, and increase the reader's connection to and empathy with the character.

➤ When encouraging re-reading: After a successful flabbergast, many readers will go back to the beginning of the narrative to hunt for clues or foreshadowing, or try to pin down how the twist happened.

➤ When challenging genre or reader expectations: This type narrative device can throw a reader for a loop, but in a good way. It can turn the tables on genre conventions and make a story filled with familiar and comfortable tropes feel new again.

➤ To set up the sequel: Nothing catapults a reader into Book 2 quite like a flabbergast.

➤ When you just know it's right for the story. If it's right, it's right; when you know, you know.

And here are some reasons to avoid using it. Yes, you'll recognize these, but they're worth repeating:

➤ It's not right for the genre.

➤ It's not right for the book.

➤ If it's predictable: If you've already used several of the same type of cliffhanger at the end of scenes throughout the story, or in other books in the series, or if it's an overly used trope in your subgenre, that might be a good reason to skip it.

➤ If it undermines the character—in other words, if the surprise contradicts your main character's previously established beliefs or behavior in a way that is unbelievable, then the reader needs some explanation. Don't leave them hanging, or they might let go.

➤ If it disrupts the tone and pacing, it may be perceived as jarring and uncomfortable. Make sure that a flabbergast makes sense both for the plot and for the structure of your story.

➤ For shock value. The very definition of flabbergasts is that they are unexpected. However, it should at least feel like it made sense for the story—even if it was an abrupt about-face.

Personally, I am a big fan of flabbergasts. I think they are fun, riveting, and emotionally engaging. However, as always, in the end it comes down to what's right for the story.

CHAPTER 7:
Threads

Most writers and readers are familiar with the idea of threads, and I think most would argue that threads don't really count as a "cliffhanger" per se.

THREADS

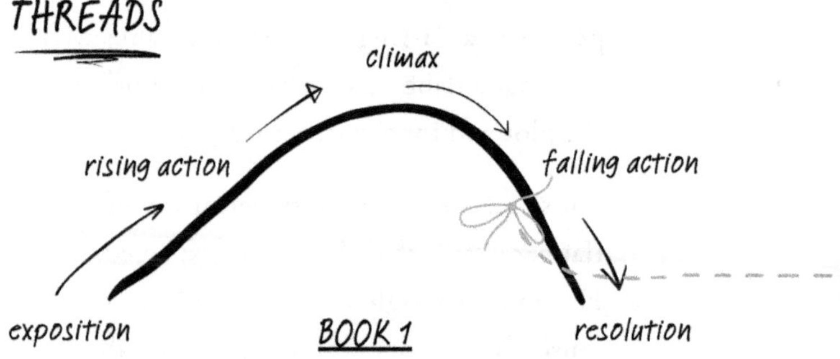

A thread, if you haven't heard the term before, is simply a question asked in one book that isn't answered until a later book. It's an idea that stretches between stories, typically related to main conflict but not always integral.

Often, threads lead to clues that slowly nudge the main character toward the key resolution for the series, or some sort of item or information they need to procure in order for the main conflict to be resolved. They may also be related to subplots and are either fully connected to the main plot, or not related at all. The longer the series, the more threads there are likely to be left hanging from book to book. A series like *The Wheel of Time* by Robert Jordan will have many threads left at the end of a book, some of them more noticeable and impactful, and some of them smaller and perhaps not noticed until much later in the series.

Many writers drop what at first appear to be tiny clues early on in a series, but end up becoming much more impactful and relevant later on. If such questions

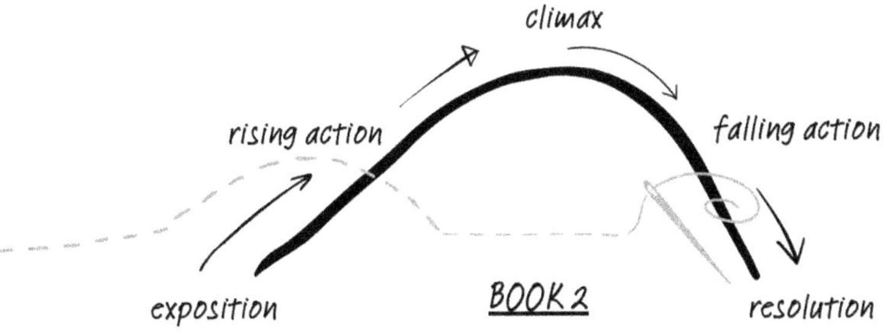

are eventually answered in a later story, even if not in Books 1 or 2, they are considered threads.

If left *un*answered, well, those are plot holes.

In this image, there are two books, each represented by its own hill. Each book has its own exposition, rising action, climax, falling action, and resolution. But there is an idea or theme or question left unanswered in the first book, represented by the needle and thread, that ties into something relevant in the second book. It might be connected to a main plot, a subplot, or the series plot, but the key here is that **the question**

is left unanswered at the end of an earlier book, but addressed in a later book.

Sometimes, a reader might notice a thread they are really interested in. I think this is common in fantasy novels with a romantic subplot. The writer will leave small, subtle clues to the romance starting to form in the first book or two of a series. But because the romance is a subplot, there isn't any resolution of the romance until a much later book.

I did this in my *Land of Szornyek* series. I had a very loose, light romantic subplot planned, and I had readers trying to guess who would end up with whom right from the beginning. I even had the main character interested in a completely different character for the entirety of Book 2, but a couple of readers noticed a potential connection between the main character and someone else in Book 1. However, this thread didn't get resolved until Book 5.

Threads are a useful storytelling technique that enable the writer to maintain tension and intrigue across numerous books in a series, and can help keep readers engaged in a longer narrative, even after the climax of a book has passed. They can be used in pretty much any series—even monadnocks, if you want. The only time to avoid them is when a book isn't in a series at all. And try to make sure they eventually get fully resolved, even if it takes a while.

CHAPTER 8:
The Fizzler

Fizzlers are not technically cliffhangers either. Rather, a fizzler is an ending that is underwhelming, disappointing, or flat. The exposition and rising action may have been exciting, entertaining, engaging—an emotional rollercoaster. But the climax? Falling action? Resolution? They just fell flat.

There are quite a few reasons these endings occur.

Subjective Fizzlers

The first reason is that the story just wasn't to the reader's taste. For what it's worth, despite all the jibber jabber in the writing community about "writing to market" or "what readers want"—there's nothing we can really do to guarantee a book hits that perfect sweet spot. Some books are going to find their readers, and some aren't. Some books will have a lot of readers; some won't.

We can read popular books and analyze them for patterns, binge entire series in the subgenres we write in, read reviews, participate in Bookstagram and Book-Tok, attend book clubs, send out surveys and whatever else you can come up with to get feedback on what readers do and don't like.

But sometimes a book will just... fall flat. To a single reader, or to a whole boatload of them.

Sometimes this is because a book gets super hyped up because it hits a spot for some readers, but it doesn't hit the spot for you (or a specific reader of your work). Sometimes the ending wasn't what you hoped—there's no happy ending, for example, or a character you liked dies. Sometimes, a love triangle turns out the opposite of what you hoped for.

Not every book is for every reader. And not every book even has that many potential readers to begin with.

And that's okay. There's one solution for this problem, and that is this: write another book. Try again. Keep at it. It's part of being a writer.

Offstage Fizzlers

Another reason for a fizzler is that either the conflict, the falling action, or the resolution happens offstage. A good example of this is *Pebble In The Sky* by Isaac Asimov. Yes, I'm going to pick on one of my favorite writers of all time. He's dead, though, so he won't get mad about it.

(Spoilers ahead!)

Pebble in the Sky is a beautifully written story that takes place in the distant future, after Earth has become radioactive. Native people from Earth are considered second-class citizens and are mostly outcasts and mutants. The story begins when Joseph Schwartz, a retired tailor from the twentieth century, is accidentally transported through time to a future version of Earth. He is then unwittingly used as a test subject for a device designed to maximize human intelligence. This device makes him hyper-intelligent and telepathic.

Schwartz slowly becomes involved in a political plot, in which a group of people is trying to exterminate all non-Earth humans in order for Earth to reclaim its glory as a dominant power in the galaxy, and their plan involves releasing a gene-targeting plague. With the help of a character named Arvardan, who is an archeologist studying Earth, as well as a woman named Pola and her father, Schwartz uses his telepathic powers to find out what's going on. Schwartz then devises a plan to prevent the plague from being released, but is thwarted at every turn, culminating in being captured.

The story is told from an omniscient, multiple-point-of-view perspective, but draws in closer on specific viewpoint characters in each scene. At the climactic moment of the book, the reader is focused on Arvardan. He makes a grand speech, trying to convince the authorities of what is going on, and then gets knocked out by a guard.

When he wakes up, he discovers that Schwartz, with his telepathic abilities, has just... fixed everything.

While everyone else was busy or unconscious, Schwartz knocked out his guard, hijacked the mind of a pilot who flew him to where the virus was being stored, and dropped a bomb on it. The virus wasn't released; problem solved.

As much as I loved the book and the absolute beauty of Asimov's prose, I found myself disappointed by the way the story was told. I remember reading Schwartz's recounting of the bombing of the laboratory where the virus was being held, and flipping back through the pages to see if I missed something. I kept thinking, *Wait, what? I wanted to be there with him! Not unconscious with Arvardan!*

For me, this was a disappointing ending. Sure, it had all the elements of a story—the exposition, the rising action, the climax, the falling action, and the resolution—but the part I wanted to see happened offstage. It was a fizzler—though still worth the read.

Lopsided Fizzlers

Have you ever played a video game where you spent hours and hours going through all the quests, leveling up your character, and fighting as many creatures as possible—only to get to the biggest boss and have it take thirty seconds to beat?

This happened to me in a game called *Torchlight II*, and as much as I loved smashing all the goblins, I was very disappointed by the final boss fight.

The problem was that it was unbalanced. The time I spent leveling up compared to the time it took me to defeat the boss was disproportionate, at least compared to my expectations.

Narratives can have the same problem. It can look like several things:

- ➤ Rushing through the ending

- ➤ Too much or not enough build-up

- ➤ The voice or style changing from the beginning to the end

- ➤ Having tons of details surrounding a subplot, but fewer surrounding a main plot

- ➤ Feeling like the main conflict was too easily resolved

At the risk of infuriating avid Harry Potter fans, I want to bring up *The Deathly Hallows* by J.K. Rowling as an example of a lopsided fizzler. The final book in the series was disappointing for one specific reason: because the author shoved too much backstory and lore into the final tome.

The question was simple: how would Harry defeat Voldemort? We knew he would, but we didn't know how, or what he would have to sacrifice along the way. The rest of the series we spent at Hogwarts, but in this book we spent most of the story in a tent in the woods.

While the lore surrounding the Deathly Hallows—the wand, the sorcerer's stone, and the invisibility cloak—was interesting, it was a *lot* compared to the rest of the series. The other six books had the relevant lore more or less woven into the story, with a focus on the relationships between the main characters and Harry's growth as a person, but the final volume was densely packed with lore-focused detail and much less focused on the characters or Harry's character arc.

Not that the other elements weren't there at all, to be clear. But it was weighted heavily toward lore, world-building, and backstory compared to the other books. Though I'm not a fan of the series anymore, I was at the time it came out, and I remember feeling like it was a part-time job to make it through the final installment of the series.

This is what I would consider a lopsided fizzler.

Series Fizzlers

You may have heard of "Second Book Syndrome," a phenomenon in which readers fall in love with a world and a character in the first book in the series, but are disappointed by how the series develops in the second book.

This is a different kind of fizzler—a multi-book fizzler, if you will.

Essentially, the promises and tension delivered by the first book are not fulfilled by the second book. This can also happen in Book 3 of a series or Book 4—or any book later in the series. Sometimes one book is a series fizzler, but the rest of the series follows through satisfactorily. Perhaps every book after the first one is a fizzler.

Perhaps it's unbalanced. Or perhaps the tone or voice has changed. Perhaps the climactic moment of Book 2 was not what the reader had hoped for—or there was an unexpected cliffhanger in Book 2.

The thing is, writing Book 2 of a series is an entirely different task than writing Book 1, and both take practice. But you can't write Book 2 until you've written Book 1, which means writers get a lot more practice writing Book 1s than writing Book 2s. It also means there are a lot of disappointing Book 2s out there.

And, as you probably know, it's not just about Books 1 and 2. Writing Book 3 differs from writing Book 2; writing Book 4 differs from writing Book 3; and writing Book 5 differs from any of the previous tales—especially in Mountain Range series. It is really challenging to keep the pacing, tension, and suspense going in just one book—let alone every book in the series!

So there are often series fizzlers—either books that have fallen to Second Book Syndrome, or books that simply did not live up to the excitement and hype of the earlier books in the series.

This is, of course, highly subjective. And some readers are far more forgiving than others. Of the reviews for my future fantasy series *Aria's Song*, some say it does not suffer from Second Book Syndrome, and others say it does.

There's nothing I can really do about that—other than to keep practicing and hope my next series is better than my last.

How To Avoid Fizzlers

I'm not sure I have any guaranteed advice for avoiding fizzlers, other than to keep practicing your craft. The thing is, sometimes you just know what's right for your story, and there can be a disconnect between what a reader expects and what you deliver. And this can keep happening. Even after writing five books or ten or fifty. That's okay.

Write more books. Write more short stories. Write longer stories and shorter ones. Write more books in more series. Get feedback on your stories, from betas, professional editors, and readers. Experiment with techniques and structures. Write some more.

Just keep at it.

Sometimes, your books will be disappointing to some readers, and that can't be predicted or avoided. It's just as likely, however, that your books will be enjoyed by other readers—this also can't always be predicted or guaranteed. All readers are not the same.

Books are complex things. A reader can enjoy one part and not another, and a different reader can enjoy exactly the opposite parts. I think that's part of why fan fiction is so popular among avid fans of various authors and stories, because they can rewrite parts of the story the way they wished it had happened.

You might love one character and the world-building but not love the ending. You might love one book in a series but not another.

I am a fan of Sylvia Mercedes' *Prince of the Doomed City* series. I didn't like Book 3 as much as I liked Books 1, 2, and 4, but you can bet I'm grabbing Book 5 as soon as it's available.

Books are complex, readers are complex, and feelings and opinions change over time. Not every book is going to be a home run; not every book is going to be a failure. Most books are going to land somewhere in the middle.

It's all okay; just keep writing.

If you were really hoping for some more practical strategies besides "keep writing," here are a few things to get you started:

➤ If you're a plotter, plan the ending before you start. Don't get started until you know how the climax fits in with the rest of the book.

➤ If you're a pantser, trust yourself. It's tough to get through an ending the first time (and the second and third, if I'm being honest) but push through, even if it doesn't make sense. And then push through the revisions. The process matters as much as the result, so do the work and figure out what works for you.

➤ If you're a plotter, consider planning the entire series in advance. Or at least plan Book 2 and 3 before drafting Book 1. If you're a pantser, consider writing Books 2 and 3 before publishing anything.

➤ Finish the project. And then finish another one. And another one.

➤ Pay attention to how the character has changed throughout the first book, and how the climactic moment is connected to their arc. Then try to pull that change into the next book.

➤ Make a list of all the conflicts and subplots in the story. Which ones are resolved? Which ones are you saving for the next book?

➤ Stay true to the theme of the story. Make sure the climax is delivering the message you want it to.

➤ Don't rush the ending. Take as much time as you need to tell the story. If it becomes too big or unwieldy, look at the beginning—what can you move to an earlier scene? Did you accidentally write two books in one? Where can you tighten up the writing? Is there a character you can eliminate?

➤ Balance the description, dialogue, and action. Include enough of each to communicate the tension, conflict, and character growth through each part of the story, without relying too heavily on one single element.

➤ Test your ending with beta readers or professional editors. What advice do they have? Remember, you don't have to agree with them or make the changes they suggest, but it can give you an idea of how readers will receive the ending.

➤ Revise, revise, revise. Study the craft of writing. Learn how you can improve your storytelling.

Writing is about communication. Communicating your narrative most effectively to your reader means studying the tactics and techniques that have worked for storytellers before you, and developing your own new and unique ways to implement them in your stories.

Don't be afraid to experiment, and don't be afraid to try again.

CHAPTER 9:
Cliffhanger vs Closure

A cliffhanger can be an effective tool for increasing suspense in a narrative. But the trick is knowing when to offer closure and when to leave your reader hanging.

The key to effective suspense is to strategically withhold information from your reader. Right from the beginning, you want them asking, "Why? Who? Where? What?"

If the narrative waits too long to answer the questions, the reader may grow bored and give up. If the narrative answers the questions too quickly, it may feel too easy, like a copout. But when the narrative feeds just enough information to keep the reader begging for more—that's where the balance is. It's like Goldilocks: not too cold, not too hot. It has to be just right.

A cliffhanger is nothing more than a technique for withholding information. In order for it to be effective, the reader has to have enough *other* information so they know exactly where something is missing. They might not know *what* is missing, but they have enough details to keep rolling forward. And they have to trust that the author is going to give them what they're looking for eventually—if not now, sooner than later.

One thing that often gets left out of conversations about writing is the idea that, throughout the course of a story, a rapport is built between the author and the reader. The author offers details, and the reader reacts to them. Preferred reactions are emotional reactions—smiles, tears, throwing the book, exclamations, laughter, or simply making the choice to keep turning page after page. Unpreferred reactions are closing the book and never picking it up again. Feeling disconnected from the narrative. Getting pulled out of the story time and time again.

As the author, we create the foundation for this rapport. And we can ask the reader questions through the narrative: What do you think of this? How should the character behave? What is the key to this puzzle?

Each time the reader answers the question in their mind, more of a rapport is established. Eventually, the reader begins to trust you. This is why you sometimes hear readers say, "Yeah, I didn't like their last book, but I'll still buy anything they write." Because they trust that author. They know that even their favorite authors have bad days—and bad books. But they keep coming back anyway—because they've established trust.

A good example of this is in the *Doctor Who* episode, "The Time of Angels." If you are unfamiliar with this TV show, *Doctor Who* follows a time-traveling alien who explores all of time and space in his spaceship, the TARDIS. The show is the longest-running science fiction TV show of all time, with the first episode originally airing in 1963. In the episode, "The Time of Angels," which aired in 2010, the Doctor and his companion, Amy, explore the wreck of the Byzantium spaceship, which has crashed into catacombs filled with Weeping Angels—a particularly terrifying alien creature that subsists on time energy.

This is a two-part episode, and the first part ends on a cliffhanger. The angels have cornered the Doctor and his companion. It seems like there is no way out. Then the Doctor, who is becoming increasingly angry as the angels kill more soldiers, tells them something along the lines of (paraphrased): "There is one thing you never put in a trap!" and the angel says, "What's that?" and the Doctor replies, "Me!" Then he shoots a gun into the air and the episode ends.

As the viewer, you don't know what's going to happen. You don't know how the Doctor and his companions are going to get out of this predicament they find themselves in. But, if you're a *Doctor Who* fan, you know you can trust the writers. You know the Doctor will get out of the trap. The question is this: *How?* And what will the consequences of their escape be?

A cliffhanger can be a strategic withholding of information, but the key here is *strategic*. Withholding information because you don't know what comes next or because you want to jerk your reader around isn't really strategic. It's important to ask yourself: Why is this necessary for the story? How will this help the reader better understand the conflict or the theme? Is there a better way to do this?

So how do you know when to leave the reader hanging and when to give them closure?

One of the toughest parts of being an adult human is working on long-term goals. It's teaching yourself how to run because you know exercise will have long-term payoffs. It's taking your vitamins every day because you know you'll probably live longer if you do. It's doing your taxes, getting your teeth cleaned, and forcing yourself through that colonoscopy prep.

It's doing things you know you should do, even though there's no reward in it for you now, or even in the foreseeable future. The rewards are nebulous, figurative, or not guaranteed—but you do it anyway.

Don't do this to your readers.

Show them their rewards. Give them a trail of breadcrumbs—or, no, not breadcrumbs. Candy. Or pizza. Or beer. Show them the beer, and promise them a fountain of beer at the end of the story.

Reward them each time they progress through the story.

The rewards are going to be different for each reader, each genre, and each story. But it could be as simple as giving them a common genre trope. In a fairy-tale retelling, maybe a fairy godmother appears. In a horror story, maybe someone hung real human skulls in the woods or a basement. In a thriller, maybe there's a car chase. In a mystery, drop a clue. In a romance novel, make the characters kiss!

There's no reason to give away the whole ending in chapter two. But each tidbit, each glimmer of the ending, leads the reader toward the fountain of beer. At least, in a bromance. In a romance, it might lead toward a sex scene. In a mystery, an arrest. In a fantasy novel, a battle scene. Or a dragon.

One of my favorite cliffhanger endings of a TV show episode is from *Person of Interest*. The show is a case study for suspense, if you've never seen it. In the show, an ex-CIA operative (Reese) and a wealthy programmer (Finch) work together to save lives by preventing crime before it even happens. They do this with information provided by a "machine" the programmer built to prevent terror attacks before they occur by predicting human behavior.

In Season 1, Episode 4, "Cura Te Ipsum," the Machine spits out the name of a young doctor who works sixteen-hour days at the hospital, and then, surprisingly, spends her evenings in clubs. Reese follows her to determine whether she is the victim or the perpetrator of the future crime. Eventually, he realizes she is hunting a man who is a serial rapist and who attacked her sister. The sister subsequently died by suicide because of the assault, and the doctor wants to exact revenge.

Once they realize what is happening, Reese sits her down and tells her not to do it. He explains that killing a person changes you. She reluctantly agrees that perhaps it is not in her best interest to murder the man, no matter what he did to her sister. But Reese and Finch aren't about to let a predator like him back out on the streets to prey on innocent women. The scene cuts to Reese sitting across the table from the rapist, Andrew, with a gun in between them. They have a conversation about ethics and morality, about what makes a good person. Andrew is pleading for his life and says, "Please, you don't want to do something you'll regret."

And Reese replies, "Which do you think I'll regret more—letting you live or letting you die?" There's a pause, and then he says, "Andrew, help me make a good decision."

Then the episode ends. And the next episode starts a new story.

While this episode might drive some viewers crazy, because you never actually find out what decision Reese made, I love it, because it ends on a question—not to Andrew, but to me, the viewer. The question is: *What is the right decision? What would a good person do?*

And then the episode lets me decide.

This is an excellent example of strategic withholding of information. It forces the viewer to think and consider the ethics of the situation. To think about morality. About what it means to be a good person.

You can't predict how a reader will respond to the choices you make in your narrative. But you can make those decisions purposefully and intentionally.

Deciding How To End The Story

Throughout this book, I've talked a lot about intentionality, about ending your narrative with purpose, even if you leave the reader on a cliff. But talk is easy; doing is hard.

But there is one strategy I have used time and time again that I've found extremely ehlpeful when I'm not quite sure what the answer is.

When don't know how to end my story, I back-plot the story.

I begin by looking at the beats I've already written, the key events that have drawn the reader from the beginning of the story to where I am now. I write them out as a list, or try to sketch out my intended flow of the tension and pacing. This often reveals the path forward.

This can work both for pantsers and plotters. Looking at the story backwards gives you an entirely different view of the story, even if you outlined it ahead of time.

Another useful method is asking questions about the narrative as a way of walking around the ending, poking at it, and seeing how it ties into the rest of the story. You can ask yourself (or your beta readers and editors, if relevant) questions like:

➤ Is this part of a series or a serial? What type— mountain range, drumlin, or monadnock?

➤ What genre am I writing in? How common/
  expected/desired are cliffhangers in
  this genre?

➤ What is the fundamental question asked at the
  beginning of the story? Did I answer it? Will I
  answer it in this book? If not, when?

➤ What are some smaller questions asked
  throughout the story? Did I answer those?
  Will I answer them? When?

➤ How would I describe the character arc of the
  main character/s? How have they changed
  since the beginning of the narrative? Why?
  How does the climactic moment relate to the
  character's internal shift?

➤ Has the setting of the narrative changed?
  How so? Have they awakened a new magic?
  Shifted to a new location? Brought down a
  government? Did I explain how and why that
  happened, and the impact of those changes?

➤ What is the inciting incident? What is the
  meet cute? What event pushes the main
  character from the normal world into the new
  world? What is the dark night of the soul?
  Which event is the climax? Falling action?
  Resolution?

> ➤ How does it feel when I reread my story? Are there any boring parts? Slow parts? Did I feel disappointed anywhere within the story? Why? And how can I fix that?

> ➤ What impact do I think a cliffhanger here will have on the reader?

There are thousands of questions you can ask to suss out any pain points in the narrative and to determine where the best point is to end the story. Maybe you'll lean into that cliffhanger, or maybe you'll decide to add a bit more denouement. It's up to you!

CHAPTER 10:
A Good Ending Starts At The Beginning

A cliffhanger is just one technique a writer can use to create suspense and tension within a narrative. In fact, how suspenseful a narrative is depends on many, many decisions throughout the whole of the story. It's about balancing the conflict with the payouts; it's about fitting the character arc to the plot, about choosing language that helps the reader fully immerse themselves in the world.

If you want to maximize the effectiveness of a cliffhanger, look no further than the rest of the book, at everything that came before. The trick is to make the reader love the characters, love the world, and feel desperate for resolution. So when you deny them that resolution, they beg for more.

Because, ultimately, the key to a suspenseful cliffhanger starts right at the beginning—with the hook.

Why does the story begin here, in this moment, with this character?

What does this first moment have to do with the end?

Why does this opening line or scene matter? And how will the ending tie back to it?

What did you promise to your reader? And how are you going to deliver on that promise?

What are the stakes? What do the characters have to lose? And what does the *reader* have to lose?

There are lots of ways to write a good hook. You can start by making a claim that the reader may agree or disagree with—yes, even in fiction! For example, "It is a truth universally acknowledged that a single man in possession of a good fortune must be in want of a wife." Sound familiar?

A few other techniques for hooks include:

- ➤ Begin by asking a question, either in prose or in dialogue. For example, "Who is John Galt?" from *Atlas Shrugged* by Ayn Rand.

- ➤ Use vivid imagery. For example, "As Gregor Samsa awoke one morning from uneasy dreams, he found himself transformed in his bed into a gigantic insect," from *Metamorphosis* by Kafka.

- ➤ Include a bold declaration, such as "Call me Ishmael," from *Moby Dick* by Herman Melville.

- ➤ Have something surprising happen. For example, "All children, except one, grow up," from *Peter Pan* by J.M. Barrie.

- ➤ Begin in the middle of things. For example, "A throng of bearded men, in sad-colored garments and gray steeple-crowned hats, intermixed with women, some wearing hoods, and others bareheaded, was assembled in front of a wooden edifice, the door of which was heavily timbered with oak, and studded with iron spikes," from *The Scarlet Letter* by Nathaniel Hawthorne.

And these are just a few examples among many.

This first moment of the narrative sets the stage for whatever happens at the end. And then each following moment is another line in the chain that keeps dragging the reader forward. It's another breadcrumb. Another piece of candy. Another beer on the path to Beer Fountain.

Most of this book has focused on the end of the story. But, truthfully, without a strong beginning, the ending doesn't mean much.

The beginning of the story needs to ask a question:

- ➤ Who is that masked man?

- ➤ How did she get here?

➤ Where are they going?

➤ Who will die along the way?

➤ Why did they do it?

➤ How is that possible?

➤ Wtf?

And the end of the story needs to answer that question—or at least it should promise an eventual answer.

If you choose to withhold answering the question by using a cliffhanger, make sure you know why. Make sure you know what you hope to achieve and what emotional experience you intend for the reader to have.

Of course, most of the time, discussions surrounding cliffhangers focus on reader preference. Will the readers enjoy a cliffhanger? Which type? Will my use of cliffhangers keep a reader on the edge of their seat, turning page after page late into the night? Send them rushing out to buy the next book?

But, ultimately, the most important factor for deciding to use a cliffhanger is this: is it right for your story? And that's a question only you can answer. You get to decide what kind of story you want to tell, and you get to decide how you want that story to end.

I know, I know. "You get to decide" sounds an awfully lot like a copout. Like I don't really know what the true key to the perfect cliffhanger is.

Well, I do.

I debated whether to include it in this book. After all, does the magician reveal their secrets? Plus, it might make a few readers mad.

But I'm nice. I shan't leave you in suspense. So here it is.

The key to crafting the most impactful cliffhangers is always ensuring that you—

READ MORE!

Hook, Line, and Cliffhanger is the fifth book in the Writer's Reach series! You can read more about writing and the business of publishing in the other books:

- ➤ *How To Build A Book Marketing Strategy*

- ➤ *The Intersection of Setting and Story*

- ➤ *Building An Author Brand That Suits You*

- ➤ *How To Pants A Novel*

- ➤ *Hook, Line, and Cliffhanger*

You can also check out Ariele's fiction work in any of the following series:

- ➤ *Aria's Song*: a complete future fantasy trilogy

- ➤ *Land of Szornyek*: a complete 7-book series of post-apocalypse with monsters (a completed series of 7)

- ➤ *Rove City*: an ongoing series of fairy tales in space

- ➤ *Zirian Chronicles*: a finished 6-book series of soft sci-fi portal fiction

- ➤ *Ariele's Fairy Tales*: an ongoing series of collections of original fairy tales exploring modern values

- ➤ *Rutherford the Unicorn Sheep*: a complete series of 8 kid's books

Finally, if you'd like, you can sign up for my newsletter to receive monthly letters on marketing, publishing, and writing, or you can join my Discord server for writers, where we chat all things writing, run sprints, and support each other in our writing careers and hobbies.

These resources are available on my page for writers: https://arielesieling.com/for-writers

ACKNOWLEDGMENTS

First, I'd like to say thank you to my writing community, Write All The Words, hosted on Discord. You provide much support and encouragement to me, and I'm grateful to you every day!

I'd also like to give a heartfelt thank you to my patrons for supporting me through the years and enabling me to continue writing books and pursing what I love.

Thank you to Cameron G., Christopher H., Josh H., John G., Gary S., Isys J., Harley O., Cullen M., Evan S., Elenaki, Phoebe D., Maria G., Kat S., Jes S., David L., Tim P., Cayce S., Robert B., Andrea KD., Eileen T., Gendermancy, and Chas M Bicking.

Patrons get every fiction book I publish included with their membership, which comes to a savings of between \$15 – 50 every year. In addition, they get custom art, sneak peeks, updates, the ability to speak directly with me, their names listed on my acknowledgments page, and more.

Finally, I want to say thank you to Josh, whose support of my career has made all this possible! 🖤

ABOUT THE AUTHOR

Ariele Sieling is a Pennsylvania-based writer who enjoys books, cats, and trees. Her first love, however, is science fiction and fantasy, and she has four series in the genres: post-apocalyptic monsters in *Land of Szornyek*; soft science fiction series, *The Zirian Chronicles*; scifi fairy-tale retellings in *Rove City*; and future fantasy trilogy, *Aria's Song*. She has numerous short stories published in a variety of anthologies and magazines, is the author of the children's books series *Rutherford the Unicorn Sheep*, and publishes non-fiction books about writing and publishing under the name A.J. Sieling.

She lives with her spouse, 160lb Great Pyrenees dog, and four cats.

You can follow Ariele by signing up for her newsletter, checking out her website, or on the social media of your choice.

Visit www.arielesieling.com for more information.